Publisher: www.sakurabookpublishing.com
alta@sakurabookpublishing.com

Illustrations :
Sanjana Singh

(Nelson & Thandi): Girisha Naicker ~ ArtGiri
girishanaicker.artist@gmail.com
Instagram: @art_giri

ISBN: 978-1-0370-5066-4(print)

978-1-0370-5067-1(e-book)

"The intense heat of summer brought a storm so fierce, that swept me off my feet in a blink of an eye. My dear husband, how do I tell you how difficult life is without you-how much I miss you."

Thandi, the elephant, sits alone at the magic pond, staring at her husband's reflection with great sadness. A tear drop falls, sliding down her cheek and onto the grass.

Nelson comes running in and comes to a sudden stop. "Umama, don't cry," he wipes his mother's tears. "Baba is with us, in our hearts. Everything will be alright."

Thandi gives off a gentle smile as she hugs her son, the biggest blessing of her life.

Thandi, along with her son Nelson, live in a small village at the foot of the Drakensberg mountains- a mountain range more than 200 kilometres long in KwaZulu-Natal.

It's the fifth summer since Thandi's husband, Simon has passed.

The mountain air is crispy

The rooster crows

Dew drops settling on the green grass and the golden sun's rays strike Nelson's face.

"Wake up Nelson, you have school."

Nelson immediately gets up. School is his favourite place. He's always been such a curious and optimistic child.

Thandi and Nelson hike to school and thereafter Thandi goes to work. She is a caretaker of the homelands.

While walking back home that day, curious little Nelson asked Thandi a question, “Umama, what’s Ubuntu?”
“Where did you hear that, Indodana(son)”

"At school. My teacher asked us to find out what Ubuntu is and give an example. That's my homework for today."

"Well you see indodana, Ubuntu means 'Humanity'. Humanity means to help someone in need and show compassion."

"Your baba was a very good soccer player. The star of our village and neighbouring villages. One day, he and his team were selected to play in a soccer tournament. The tournament was held in KwaDukuza, a town that's about 4 hours away. Your baba and his team stayed there for a week and on the day, they were supposed to return home, an accident took place ."

The unbearable summer heat led to flooding throughout KZN. Our land was destroyed. We were unable to farm for months. Many homes in the low-lying areas got washed away. The towns and cities weren't spared either. Many roads were damaged and bridges collapsed.

"Simon and his team were on the bus when it got swept away by the flooding. Some of his team members managed to escape despite the serious injuries, but Simon was trapped. His team was in no condition to have the strength to help him. People tried helping those in need but attended to the non-African elephants first. Your father waited and waited, shouting out for help but he was ignored. We almost lost him, son."

Nelson gasps, "And then what happened?"

"A kind white elephant immediately rushed to your father's aid once he was spotted."

The white elephant saved Simon and took him safely to a camp for the flood survivors. The flood survivors were given medical treatment.

Baba was grateful to the white elephant for saving him despite being of different colour skin.
The elephant showed Ubuntu.

"I am going to speak to my class about my father's story."

Thandi smiles proudly.

"Come on, lets get going. It's getting late."

Thandi and Nelson continue walking home while remembering moments spent with Simon.

Dusk settled in, but Nelson didn't return home. Thandi grew worried, pacing back and forth.

"Hey Siya!", she calls out to a boy of around Nelson's age that was playing nearby.

"Sawubona, Aunty."

"Sawubona Unjani, have you seen Nelson? He has not returned home from school."

"He left school as soon as the bell rang. He was crying a lot. I thought he would've come straight home."

"Why was he crying?", asks Thandi, growing even more anxious.

"I heard from the kids in his class that a group of boys made fun of him. They mocked him for his skin colour and one of the boys even used him as an example of Ubuntu. He said that you were kind enough to take him under your care. That horrible boy also said that you pity Nelson because his real parents abandoned him. All the kids in his class pointed fingers at him and called him 'Ubuntu boy'. Everyone laughed at him."

Thandi's heart sinks when she hears this. Her eyes well up as she tries to hold back her tears, but is unable to.

"Thank you, boy. You can go now." She pats him on the shoulder and he runs off.

Petrified, Thandi began searching for her son with the help of a few villagers. He was nowhere to be found in the village. It's been two hours now.

"Friend, why don't you go back home. Perhaps Nelson has already returned home", says a soft-spoken lady to Thandi.

Hopeful, Thandi rushes to her cave. When she enters, she spots little Nelson curled up in a ball under the wooden table. Teardrops roll down his cheeks, his eyes are puffy and red. It seems he's been crying for quite some time.

Thandi kneels on the floor next to the table and puts forward her hand to him. "Come here, my sweet boy. Come to Umama"

"You are not my mother!" Nelson lashes out, shoving her trunk away.

Nelson's words pierced through Thandi's heart like a spear. "What do you mean ,I'm not your mother?" asks Thandi sternly

"That's what the boys in my new school said to me." Nelson wipes another tear. "When I told them that they are lying," a girl blurted out: 'Then why is your skin colour different from hers?'

Thandi pulls him out from underneath the table and makes him sit on her lap. She pulls him closer in an embrace, his head on her chest- the sobbing continues

Nelson falls asleep in his mother's trunk.

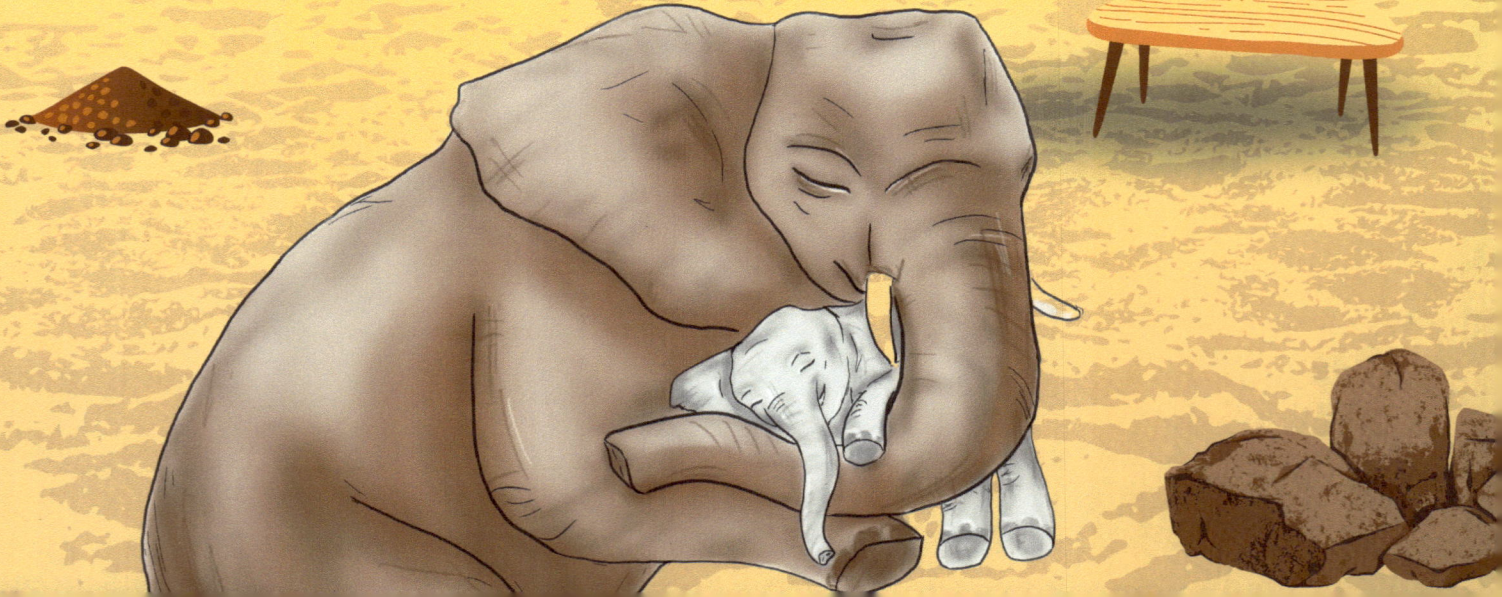

Thandi's best friend Pume, who so happens to also be her sister-in-law from the neighbouring village, came over for some tea.

Pume notices the worry on Thandi's face.

"Look, you can't keep Nelson away from the world. He is bound to find out the truth someday. Somehow, you managed to hide everything from him. The village will always support you. Everybody loves Nelson as if he were their own. He is a growing child. It's natural to have these questions."

"Have I made the wrong decision in sending him to a new school in the town?" She's trembling with anxiety.

"Absolutely not, Thandi! Nelson's education is important. Our village does not have a primary school and Nelson needs to continue with his schooling. Do not doubt your decisions. You have to be strong. You have our support. If Nelson does not understand, we will try to reason with him. That I promise you, my friend.
But tomorrow, you need to be honest with him. He will continue asking questions and you cannot avoid his questions forever. "

Thandi sighs, "I guess you're right. Thank you, my friend."
Pume bids Thandi farewell.

Thandi remains seated. Anxious, worried, scared.
She stays awake throughout the night, lost in her thoughts.

With a new morning, comes a ray of hope. The hope that Thandi will muster
the courage to tell her beloved son the truth.

"Good morning, Indodana."

Nelson wakes.

He does not say a word to his mother. He freshens up while Thandi prepares breakfast.

Nelson walks towards the entrance of the cave to leave.

"Stop my child. Come here. I will answer every question that is on your mind."

Nelson sits beside his mother.
"Will you really tell me everything?"
"Yes Indodana, I will. I promise."

Thandi takes a deep breath, pauses for a second, and then exhales. She takes his trunk in hers.

"The truth is that you are my son and I am your mother. I have not given birth to you ,but that does not change anything. Your skin colour is lighter than mine and everybody in this village because your birth parents were whites. They did not abandon you, child. They were involved in an accident and did not survive. I worked for them for many years. They were very kind elephants. They showed a lot of affection towards me. Your birth mother made me make a promise to her at the hospital before dying."

"Nelson, my dear. We live in South Africa. A country so rich in diversity and cultures.A rainbow nation. Despite the gruesome past that our forefathers have experienced, today, in present day South Africa, we stand united. Apartheid has been abolished. We don't differentiate between our skin colours. Yes, there are still some people who are stuck in the past that bring up racial division and unfortunately teach their kids the same. But let their words fall on deaf ears. I've always taught you to be resilient despite the adversity, have I not?"
Nelson nods in agreement with Thandi.

Thandi continues. "People will say nasty things ,but it your choice whether you want to ignore them or let their bitterness affect you. You live in such a supportive community. The villagers adore you, Nelson.
Have I, your father or anyone in the village ever make you feel as if you don't belong here?"

"No ma."

"Then?"

Nelson hugs Thandi and mumbles, "but they're calling me Ubuntu boy. What do I do?"

"You stand up to them Indodana. You fight. Not with your fists, but with your words. Choose Ubuntu.
Always remember that there is nothing in this world that can change the bond we share nor your identity! Your skin colour makes no difference."

She caresses his head with her trunk.

"Umama, how come you don't have your own child? A child that you birthed?"

Thandi is stunned by this question. A question she did not expect Nelson to ask, at least not at this moment.

A tear escaped from her eye, onto Nelsons cheek. He lifts his head up, looking at Thandi. She smiles.
"Ma, why are you crying and smiling? Are you feeling happy or sad?" asks confused little Nelson.
"I'm overwhelmed."
Nelson holds his confused expression while Thandi laughs.

"Oh, dear child, I'm grateful. I'm grateful to your father for protecting me and trying to keep me safe. He loved me so much."
"Then why didn't you both have a baby?"
"That's because your father was very sickly."

"Do you remember, last year some people from the town came to the village. They held a campaign on HIV/Aids. They handed out flyers, educating people about this illness."

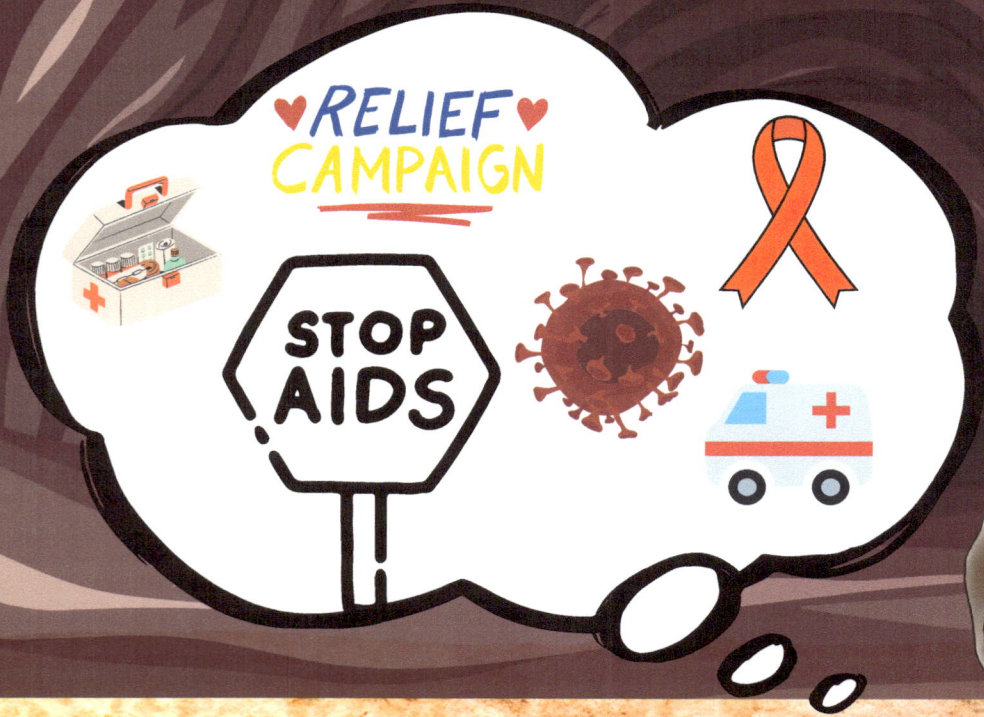

Nelson quickly runs to his wooden chest and takes out a small red badge with the shape of a ribbon crossed over and shows it to Thandi.

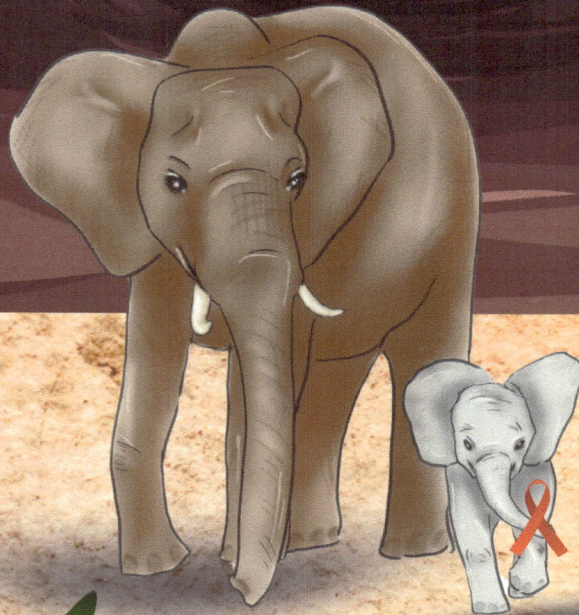

"Did baba have HIV/Aids?" he asks softly.

"Yes, he did. When he was taken to the refugee camp during the summer floods, he contracted the illness. I'm sure your teacher might have told you that South Africa is a hotspot for HIV/Aids in the world. We have the highest number of infected people."

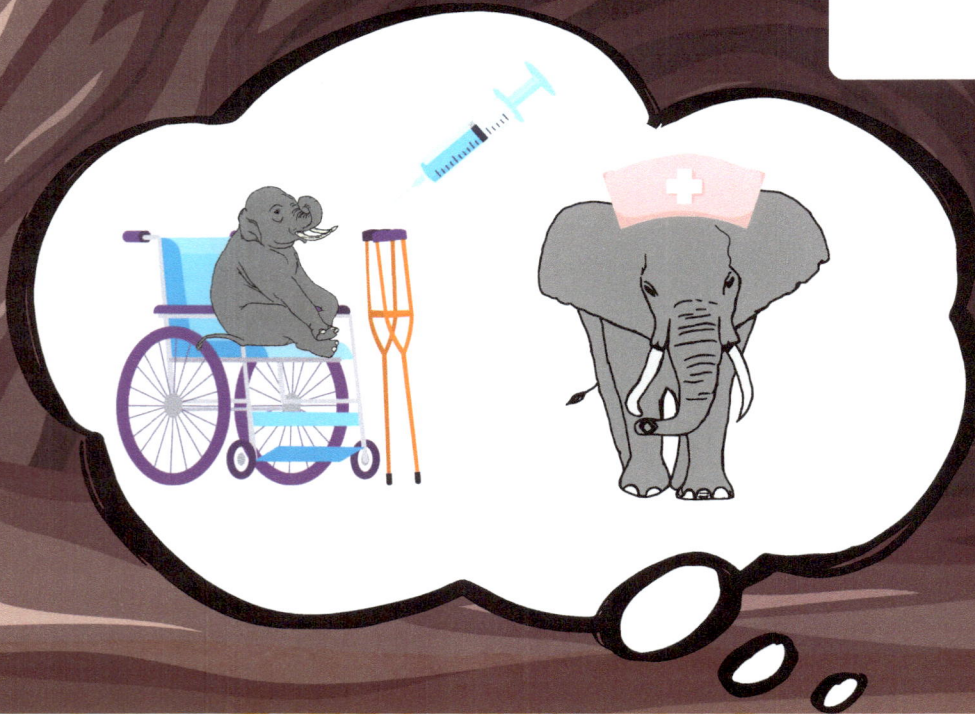

"Over time, he became sickly. One day, when I had taken him to the clinic, we found out that he was HIV positive. With the assistance of the clinic, he survived much longer than expected. He had his routine check-ups and education on how to take care of himself was provided, through community drives. Simon made sure not to pass on the illness to me. He tried his best to keep me safe."

"How did he do that ?"

"At school, did the teacher explain how HIV/Aids is spread?"
"Yes ma, she explained briefly"

"Good, so your father protected me by keeping away from me physically. Therefore, we could not have a child of our own."

"I'm sorry, ma."
"Why are you sorry?"
"You couldn't have a child."
"But I'm not sorry, son. I have a child. You're my child. My greatest blessing and I am forever thankful to God for sending you to me.

It's a new day. A new beginning. Thandi feels lighter after getting the truth off her chest, which was weighing her down. From here on, she needs to not fear losing Nelson because honesty is the best policy.

The sun is shining, accompanied by a few wispy cirrus clouds that seem like candyfloss in the azure sky.

Nelson decides to help out in the fields along with some of the men and women, even kids of around his age. The ground is moist from the heavy summer rainfall . Everybody needs to work together. There's lots of chattering , laughter and singing on the fields, echoing in the Drakensberg mountains.

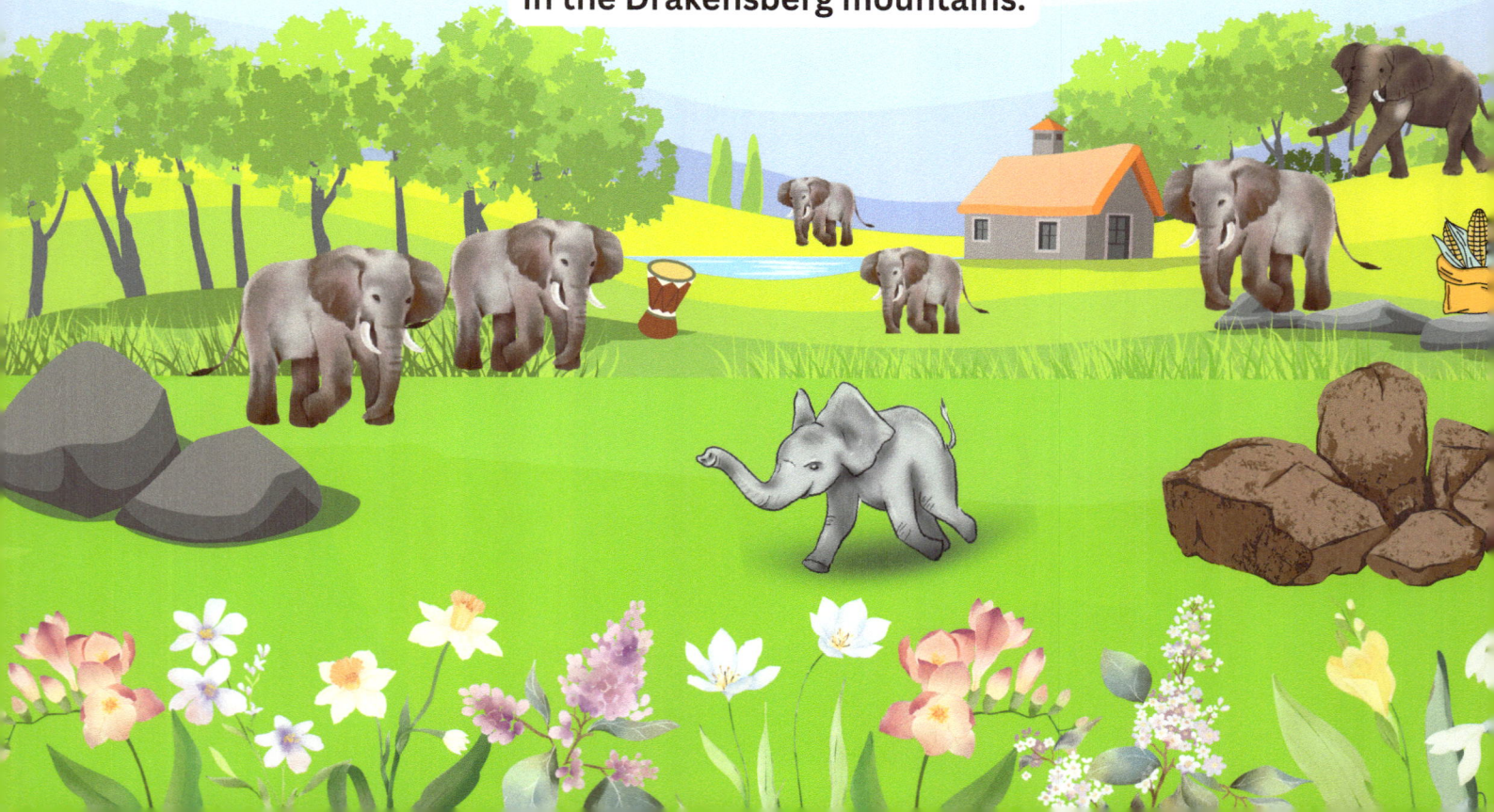

Whilst working, an elderly rude man taunts Nelson.

"You may stay in the blistering sun, child, maybe you'll start looking like one of us but you will never be one of us."

Silence is golden.
Nelson throws the rake in a fit of rage.
He clenches his fist and stomps his feet.

"I am one of you. I am African. My skin colour does not matter.
Ubuntu, malume (uncle)! Ubuntu.
I am a symbol of Ubuntu.
My mother took me in and raised me.
She showed the same humanity towards me that was shown to my father.

I grew up amongst the Zulu tribe!
I eat the same food as you!
I live the same life style!
I speak the same language!

I am proud of who I am.

You can never take away my identity from me."

The
End

About the Author

Sanjana Singh (22) is a young author in South Africa. Formally from a northern KwaZulu-Natal, currently residing in Mpumalanga. She is passionate about writing, well-versed in creative arts, with a knack for writing from various perspectives. Sanjana's work has been featured in several notable publications, however Nelson is her debut.
When she is not creating characters, she's reading about or splashing them on a canvas.

Glossary

Abolished - to end or stop something completely.

Abstained- to stop oneself from doing or enjoying something.

Adversity - a difficult situation.

Anxiety - feeling of fear or worry that happens as a response to real or perceived threats.

Assistance- to help someone by sharing work.

Azure- bright blue

Blistering- very hot

Briefly- saying something using a few words

Compassion- to show kindness and care.

Differentiate-to recognize what makes someone or something different

Diversity- means differences. People can be different in many ways.

Exhales- breathe out.

Gruesome- something terrible.

HIV/AIDS- HIV is a small germ that causes Aids. Aids is a disease that makes people very sick. There is no cure.

Glossary

Indodana- son
Mocked - to be made fun of.
Optimistic- being hopeful about the future.
Overwhelmed- feeling too strong emotions.
Pity- feeling sad for others.
Refugee camp - a camp set up to protect and help people.
Resilient- able to recover quickly from hard conditions.
Sawubona - Hello.
Sawubona Unjani - Hello, how are you?
Sobbing - Crying.
Umama - Mother.

www.ingramcontent.com/pod-product-compliance
Lightning Source LLC
Chambersburg PA
CBHW060813090426

42737CB00002B/57